WAR MOTHER

WAR MOTHER

WIN DOCKERY

J MERRILL

J MERRILL

For permission requests, please contact the Permissions Coordinator at:

J Merrill Publishing, Inc.
434 Hillpine Drive, Suite 100
Columbus, OH 43207
www.JMerrill.pub

Library of Congress Control Number: 2025909381
Paperback ISBN-13: *978-1-961475-38-0*
eBook ISBN-13: *978-1-961475-39-7*

Book Title: *War Mother*
Author: *Win Dockery*

Prayer Topics

Motherhood: A Spiritual Battle

Motherhood is something that you can't be conditioned for. You are literally thrown into a war zone from the time they are born—sometimes even as they are forming in your womb. Some things will hit you like a blow to the gut, knocking the very breath out of you. This is a fight that Dad and you are in together—or not. Either way, this isn't a fight that can be fought passively. This is a war that demands your full attention and unshakable faith.

If Dad is present, this requires both of you to be on the same page, or your fight will seem uphill. But remember that Christ is for you, and through Him, all things are possible.

There is something incredibly powerful in a mother's war cry. It is a sound that reverberates through the heavens—a cry that nurtures, protects, and stands unyielding in the face of the enemy! A mother's battle is unique, anointed by God to shape the very foundation of the next generation.

And let me tell you, if you think for one second that you're not in a war for your children, your home, and your future, you are gravely mistaken.

When you think about this book, think about any heavy artillery used in war. It is more powerful than anything the enemy can throw at you. The Word of God is our most powerful weapon, and we are equipped to use it.

You are armed and ready.
Let's go to war, sis!

A Prayer Against
Abandonment

Heavenly Father,
I come before You in the name of Jesus, lifting up my precious child(ren) to You. I thank You for the blessing of their lives and the gift of being their parent. Lord, I ask that You surround them with Your precious love and protection, especially in this time of uncertainty and feelings of abandonment.

Father, Your Word promises that You will never leave nor forsake us. I claim that promise over my child(ren)—that they will feel Your constant presence and know that You are always with them.

When they face moments of loneliness and rejection, may they remember that You, Father, are their refuge and strength, a very present help in times of trouble. Let them never forget that their value is not determined by the opinions or actions of others, but by the love You have for them. For Your Word says:

> *"For I am convinced that neither death nor life, neither*
> *angels nor demons, neither the present nor the future,*
> *nor any powers, neither height nor depth, nor*
> *anything else in all creation, will be able to separate us*
> *from the love of God that is in Christ Jesus our Lord."*

— Romans 8:38–39 (NIV)

Jehovah Rapha, heal any wounds of abandonment that may be in their heart. Abba Father, teach them to depend only on You. Let them find their identity and security in You. Help them to understand that no matter what happens in life, You are with them and for them, and You will never fail them.

I declare that my child(ren) are loved, accepted, and cherished by You, Lord. Let them walk in confidence like never before, standing in and on Your promises, knowing they are never alone, for You are always by their side.

In Jesus' name, Amen.

A Prayer for Angelic Protection

Heavenly Father, Lord of Hosts,

I come before You in the name of Jesus, thanking You for the gift of my child(ren) and the plans You have for their lives. I thank You that everything I need to steward my child(ren) has already been provided. I also thank You for the power of activation.

Today, I call upon Your living Word, which promises that You have assigned angels at birth to watch over us.

Your Word says in Psalm 91:11:

> *"For He will command His angels concerning you to
> guard you in all your ways."*

Lord, I ask You to dispatch Your angels to guard my child(ren) in every aspect of their lives. Let them walk under divine protection as they go about their days—shielded from harm, danger, and the attacks of the enemy.

I stand on the promises of Matthew 18:10, where Jesus said that the angels of children always see the face of the Father in heaven. I declare that my child(ren) are surrounded by angels who minister to them, guide them, and protect them—ensuring that no weapon formed against them will prosper.

Father, I ask that their angels go before them, making their paths straight and safe. Let Your heavenly hosts fight for them in unseen realms, as You did for Your people in Exodus 14:19–20, where the angel of God protected the Israelites by standing between them and their enemies.

May Your angels strengthen them when they feel weak, encourage them when they are discouraged, and keep them on the path You have ordained for their lives. Surround them with peace and comfort, and may they always feel Your divine presence through the work of Your angels.

Lord, I entrust my child(ren) into Your care, knowing that Your angels encamp around those who fear You.

Thank You for Your faithfulness, love, and protection.

In Jesus' name, Amen.

GUARDIANS OF REST: A PRAYER FOR MY CHILDREN'S BEDROOMS

Heavenly Father,
I come before You with thanksgiving for the gift of my child(ren) and the blessing of their lives. I dedicate their rooms to You as spaces of peace, safety, and joy.
I pray that Your presence will dwell here, just as You have promised:

> *"The Lord bless you and keep you; the Lord make His face shine upon you and be gracious to you; the Lord turn His face toward you and give you peace."*

> — NUMBERS 6:24–26

May Your peace fill every corner of this room, driving out all fear and worry.
Lord, I declare that:

> *"No weapon formed against them shall prosper."*
> *—Isaiah 54:17*

Protect their hearts, minds, and spirits from anything that would seek to harm or distract them from Your purpose. Surround this space with Your angels, as You have said:

> *"He will command His angels concerning you to guard*
> *you in all your ways."*
> *—Psalm 91:11*

Father, I pray that this room will be a place where they experience Your love and learn to grow in wisdom, stature, and favor with You and with others (Luke 2:52).

Let them hear Your voice and feel Your presence, as You promise in Jeremiah 29:13:

> *"You will seek me and find me when you seek me with all*
> *your heart."*

I speak life and truth over their dreams and thoughts. Let their rest be sweet, as You have said in Proverbs 3:24:

> *"When you lie down, you will not be afraid; when you lie*
> *down, your sleep will be sweet."*

Grant them creativity, focus, and joy in all they do.

Father, may their rooms be filled with love, hope, and faith. Help them always to know their identity in You, as they are:

> *"Fearfully and wonderfully made."*
> *—Psalm 139:14*

Remind them daily of Your plans for their lives—plans to prosper them and not to harm them, plans to give them a hope and a future (Jeremiah 29:11).

Thank You, Lord, for Your protection and guidance. I entrust their rooms, their hearts, and their futures into Your hands.

In the mighty name of Jesus, I pray, Amen.

A Prayer for Confidence

Heavenly Father,
I come to You today, lifting up my child(ren) into Your loving care. Lord, I pray for their confidence—not a confidence in the world, but a confidence that is firmly grounded in You.

Your Word says in Philippians 4:13:

> *"I can do all things through Christ which strengtheneth me."*

Help my child(ren) understand that their strength and courage come from You and that they can face any challenge with Your power working within them.

Father, I ask that You silence the lying voices of fear, doubt, and insecurity in their hearts now, in the mighty name of Jesus! Your Word says that You have not given them a spirit of fear, but of power and a sound mind (2 Timothy 1:7). May this truth give them the boldness to step into their purpose and to believe in the gifts and talents You have given them.

Help them to see themselves as You see them—fearfully and wonderfully made, just as You declare in Psalm 139:14.

Let them celebrate who they are, knowing that they were created by Your hands, on purpose, and for a purpose.

Father, allow them to walk in humility and assurance, knowing that they are never alone. Remind them of Your promise in Deuteronomy 31:6:

> *"Be strong and courageous. Do not be afraid or terrified because of them, for the Lord your God goes with you; He will never leave you nor forsake you."*

When they face challenges, encourage them to lean on You, Lord, as their source of strength. Let them confidently declare, as in Psalm 27:1:

> *"The Lord is my light and my salvation—whom shall I fear? The Lord is the stronghold of my life—of whom shall I be afraid?"*

I thank You, Lord, for the work You are doing in their lives. May they walk in confidence, knowing that they are loved, chosen, and equipped by You for every good work.

In Jesus' name, Amen.

Covering: A Prayer of Protection

Heavenly Father,

I come before You with gratitude for the precious lives of my child(ren). I thank You for their unique gifts, personalities, and the plans You have for them. Today, I lift each one of them to You—those in school and my little one at home—and I ask for Your covering, guidance, and protection over their lives.

Lord, Your Word promises in Isaiah 54:13:

> *"All your children will be taught by the Lord, and great will be their peace."*

I pray that You will guide them in their learning, both in school and in life, and fill them with Your peace as they navigate each day.

For my child(ren) in school, I ask for Your protection. Psalm 91:11 declares:

> *"For He will command His angels concerning you to guard you in all your ways."*

Lord, place a hedge of protection around them as they travel, learn, and interact with others. Guard their hearts, minds, and bodies from any harm or negative influences.

Give them wisdom and understanding, as promised in James 1:5:

> *"If any of you lacks wisdom, let him ask of God, who gives*
> *to all liberally and without reproach, and it will be*
> *given to him."*

Help them to excel in their studies and to develop the skills and knowledge they need for the futures You have planned for them.

For my youngest, I pray that You surround them with love, joy, and safety. Let them grow in health, strength, and confidence, knowing they are:

> *"Fearfully and wonderfully made."*
> *—Psalm 139:14*

Let their innocence and curiosity be preserved as they grow in Your timing and in Your care.

Father, I pray over their friendships and relationships. May they be surrounded by people who uplift and encourage them, and may they be a light to others—showing kindness, respect, and love. Protect their hearts from any feelings of rejection or negativity, and fill them with the knowledge of their worth in You.

I declare Jeremiah 29:11 over their lives:

> *"For I know the plans I have for you," declares the Lord,*
> *"plans to prosper you and not to harm you, plans to*
> *give you hope and a future."*

Help them to walk boldly in the purpose You have for them, trusting in Your guidance and provision every step of the way.

Lord, strengthen me as their parent to guide them in Your truth, to be patient and understanding, and to reflect Your love in all that I do.

Thank You for Your faithfulness and for watching over my family. I trust in Your promises and commit my child(ren) to Your care.

In the mighty name of Jesus, I pray, Amen.

DENOUNCE AND RENOUNCE

Yahweh Sabaoth, the Lord of Armies,
I come before You in the mighty name of Jesus, declaring Your Word over my child(ren) and standing in authority against every demonic force that seeks to influence or harm them. I renounce any assignment of the enemy and break every chain of darkness that has attempted to bind their mind, heart, and spirit.

Your Word says in Ephesians 6:12:

> *"For we wrestle not against flesh and blood, but against*
> *principalities, against powers, against the rulers of the*
> *darkness of this world, against spiritual wickedness in*
> *high places."*

I command every demonic force, known and unknown, to release my child(ren) now in the name of Jesus Christ! I plead the blood of Jesus over them, and I ask You, Father, to cover them with Your protection.

I claim the promise of Isaiah 54:17:

> *"No weapon that is formed against thee shall prosper; and*

every tongue that shall rise against thee in judgment
thou shalt condemn. This is the heritage of the
servants of the Lord, and their righteousness is of me,
saith the Lord."

I declare that they are free from the snares of the enemy and are covered by the blood of Yeshua. Father, I replace every demonic influence with Your holy presence and spiritual strength.

I declare the spirit of wisdom, understanding, counsel, might, knowledge, and the fear of the Lord upon my child(ren), as promised in Isaiah 11:2.

I speak peace, joy, and righteousness into their lives, as You have called them to live in Your kingdom of light. I ask Your angels to surround them and guard them in all their ways, as promised in Psalm 91:11.

Your Word declares in Romans 8:37:

> *"Nay, in all these things we are more than conquerors*
> *through him that loved us."*

I ask that Your Holy Spirit lead and guide them daily, that they may grow in grace and knowledge of You, fulfilling the plans You have set for their lives.

Father, I thank You for victory over the enemy and the power of Your Word. I speak life, strength, and faith over my child(ren) in the name of Jesus.

Amen.

A Prayer Over
Friendships

H eavenly Father,
    I come before You with gratitude for the precious lives of my child(ren). Thank You for blessing them with opportunities to build meaningful relationships. I lift up their friendships to You, asking for guidance, protection, and wisdom in every connection they form.

Your Word says in Proverbs 13:20:

> *"He that walketh with wise men shall be wise: but a*
> *companion of fools shall be destroyed."*

I pray that You surround my child(ren) with wise, loving, and godly friends who will encourage them to walk in Your truth. Help them to discern the difference between friendships that bring life and those that bring harm.

Father, I ask that You remove any friends or influences in their lives that are not from You—those that could lead them away from Your path or cause harm to their spiritual, emotional, or physical well-being.

Your Word says in 1 Corinthians 15:33:

> *"Be not deceived: evil communications corrupt good manners."*

Protect their hearts and minds, Lord, and give them the courage to walk away from any relationship that isn't healthy or aligned with Your will.

May they embody the qualities of love described in 1 Corinthians 13:4–7—patience, kindness, humility, and forgiveness. Teach them to love their friends well and to be a reflection of Your love in every relationship.

I pray for unity and peace in their friendships, as You have called us to be peacemakers. Let there be no place for jealousy, gossip, or strife, but instead, let them encourage one another and build each other up, as You instruct in 1 Thessalonians 5:11:

> *"Wherefore comfort yourselves together, and edify one another, even as also ye do."*

Lord, for the times they may feel lonely or hurt, remind them of Your promise in Psalm 68:6:

> *"God setteth the solitary in families: he bringeth out those which are bound with chains."*

Comfort their hearts and provide them with the friends they need in every season. And most importantly, help them always to know that You, Jesus, are their closest and most faithful Friend.

Thank You for Your protection over their hearts and the relationships they build. May their friendships bring glory to Your name and help them grow into the people You've called them to be.

In Jesus' name, Amen.

A Prayer for Hormonal Changes

Heavenly Father,
I come before You, humbly lifting my child(ren) into Your loving hands. Thank You for entrusting me to guide them on their life journey and to nurture them. I know that You have fearfully and wonderfully made them, knitting them together in my womb, and that Your plans for their life are good and full of hope.

Lord, I pray over their body, mind, and spirit. You know every detail of their growth and development, including the changes and challenges they may face as their hormones shift and mature. I ask for Your divine guidance in their life, that every part of their being would function according to the perfect design You intended. Where there may be imbalance or struggles, bring healing, stability, and peace, for You are Jehovah Rapha, the God who heals.

Help my child know that their worth comes from You alone. Remind them they are Your masterpiece, created in Christ Jesus to do good works. Guard their path of righteousness for Your name's sake.

Lord, I ask that You protect my child(ren) from confusion, insecurity, or fear during this season of change. Instead, fill them with the fruit of the Spirit—love, joy, peace, patience, kindness, faithfulness, gentleness, and self-control (Galatians 5:22–23). Help them to respond to their emotions and circumstances in ways that honor You.

As their mother, Lord, give me wisdom and patience to nurture and guide them through this journey. Help me to model grace, understanding, and unconditional love, reflecting Your heart in how I speak and care for them. When I feel uncertain, overwhelmed, or unequipped, remind me that You are with me, giving me strength and wisdom to lead them in Your ways.

I thank You for hearing my prayer and for loving my child(ren) more than I ever could. I trust You to work in their life for their good and Your glory. May they always know that they are deeply loved, especially by You.

In Jesus' name, Amen.

A Prayer for Godly Influence

Heavenly Father,

I come before You today with a grateful heart for the precious gift of my child(ren). I do not take lightly the task of leading and guiding them in Your ways. Lord, I lift my child(ren) to You, praying that they would grow to be a godly influence in this world—even now.

Your Word says in 1 Timothy 4:12:

> *"Let no man despise thy youth; but be thou an example of the believers, in word, in conversation, in charity, in spirit, in faith, in purity."*

I pray that even as a child, my son/daughter would shine as an example to others—speaking words of kindness, walking in love, and demonstrating purity of heart and mind.

Father, guard their heart and mind against the influence of evil. Your Word promises in Romans 12:2:

> *"And be not conformed to this world: but be ye transformed by the renewing of your mind, that ye may*

prove what is that good, and acceptable, and perfect,
will of God."

Renew their mind daily with Your truth, so they will not be drawn to what is wrong or harmful but will stand firm in what is good, pure, and pleasing to You.

Lord, help my child to surround themselves with wise and godly influences, for Your Word says in Proverbs 13:20:

"He that walketh with wise men shall be wise: but a
companion of fools shall be destroyed."

Place mentors, friends, and examples in their lives who will encourage them to walk in righteousness and help them discern what aligns with Your will. I pray that the gifts of discernment and wisdom would rest heavily upon their life.

I declare that my child(ren) will be a leader, not a follower of destructive paths. Your Word says in Jeremiah 29:11:

"For I know the thoughts that I think toward you, saith the
Lord, thoughts of peace, and not of evil, to give you an
expected end."

May their life be a light, drawing others closer to You. May they have boldness and courage to stand for Your truth and righteousness, even when it is hard.

Father, I pray that their influence will extend far beyond what I can imagine. May they speak life into their peers, inspire friends, and glorify You in all they do. As they grow, may their love for You deepen, and may they fulfill every purpose You have set before them.

Lord, You are faithful and able to complete the good work You have begun in them (Philippians 1:6). May darkness have no record of them, and may they always be known in heaven for their faithfulness to You.

In Jesus' name, Amen.

A Prayer Against Jealousy

Heavenly Father,
I come before You with a heart full of love and concern for my child(ren). Lord, You know their hearts better than I do, and You see every emotion, struggle, and thought they experience. I lift them to You today, asking that You would guard their hearts against the destructive spirit of jealousy.

Your Word says in James 3:16:

> *"For where envying and strife is, there is confusion and every evil work."*

Father, I pray that jealousy will not take root in their hearts or cause strife in their life. Instead, fill them with a spirit of love, humility, and contentment that leaves no room for jealousy.

Lord, help my child to understand that every good and perfect gift comes from You and that You have a unique plan and purpose for their life. Teach them to celebrate the blessings and successes of others, knowing that their time and blessings are in Your hands.

Your Word tells us in Romans 12:15:

"Rejoice with them that do rejoice, and weep with them that weep."

I release to You any tendency to compare or envy. Replace feelings of lack with confidence in Your provision. Remind them that they will lack nothing, for You are Jehovah Jireh, their provider.

Father, if I have unknowingly contributed to their feelings of insecurity, show me where I need to change. Help me to affirm them in their identity, worth, and purpose. Where jealousy has already crept in, I ask for Your healing. Break every chain of bitterness and replace it with joy.

Let my child walk in confidence, knowing that You have equipped them for every good work (Ephesians 2:10).

Thank You, Lord, for hearing my prayer and for covering my child(ren) with Your love and protection. I trust You to uproot jealousy and replace it with Your perfect peace.

In Jesus' name, Amen.

A Prayer Against Rebellion

Heavenly Father,

I come before You with a humble heart, seeking Your guidance and intervention in my child(ren)'s life. Lord, I see rebellion rising in their heart, and it grieves me, but I know You are a loving and merciful Father who is able to restore and transform. I lift them to You now, trusting in Your power to break the chain of rebellion and bring them back into alignment with Your will.

Your Word says in Ephesians 6:1–3:

> *"Children, obey your parents in the Lord: for this is right. Honour thy father and mother; which is the first commandment with promise; That it may be well with thee, and thou mayest live long on the earth."*

I pray that my child will come to understand the importance of obedience and honor—not just for me but ultimately for You.

Father, Your Word also says in Proverbs 22:15:

> *"Foolishness is bound in the heart of a child; but the rod of correction shall drive it far from him."*

Give me wisdom and stamina as I discipline them in love so that my actions reflect Your truth and grace. Help me to correct them in a way that leads to understanding, repentance, and restoration.

Lord, I pray against any spirits of rebellion, pride, or disobedience that seek to take hold of my child's heart. Your Word says in James 4:7:

> *"Submit yourselves therefore to God. Resist the devil, and*
> *he will flee from you."*

I declare that my child will submit to You and resist the temptations and lies of the enemy.

Holy Spirit, I ask that You work in their heart to soften it. Replace their stubbornness with a willingness to listen and learn. Replace pride with humility, anger with peace, and defiance with a desire to do what is right.

Your Word says in Ezekiel 36:26:

> *"A new heart also will I give you, and a new spirit will I*
> *put within you: and I will take away the stony heart*
> *out of your flesh, and I will give you a heart of flesh."*

I claim this promise over my child(ren) and ask that You transform their heart to be tender and responsive to Your voice.

Father, I trust in Your Word, which says in Proverbs 22:6:

> *"Train up a child in the way he should go: and when he is*
> *old, he will not depart from it."*

I have sown seeds of truth and love into their life, and I pray those seeds will take root and grow. Even if they stray for a time, I trust that they will be drawn back to You.

I release fear and worry into Your unchanging hands, knowing that You are faithful. Help me to be a reflection of Your love, grace, and steadfastness as a parent through this season.

In Jesus' name, Amen.

A Prayer Against Rejection

Heavenly Father,
    I place my child at Your feet, knowing that You are the source of their strength and comfort.

Father, You see every tear, every hurt, and every moment of rejection they face. I ask for Your peace to consume them, Your truth to fill their heart, and Your love to anchor their soul. Remind them, Lord, that rejection from man does not define their worth, for their identity is secure in You.

Your Word says in Psalm 118:22:

> *"The stone which the builders refused is become the head
> stone of the corner."*

Just as You turned rejection into a foundation for greatness in Jesus' life, help my child(ren) to see that rejection can be part of Your divine plan. May they trust that Your ways are higher than their ways and Your thoughts higher than their thoughts (Isaiah 55:8–9).

Lord, I declare over my child(ren) that when one door closes, You are preparing a better one to open. The only reason it closed in the first place is because You allowed it. Shield them from bitterness, and help them to see that rejection can be Your protection.

Your Word promises in Romans 8:28:

> *"And we know that all things work together for good to them that love God, to them who are the called according to his purpose."*

May they rest in the assurance that You are always working for their good.

Give them Your wisdom to discern where You are leading, strength to walk in obedience, and courage to rise above disappointment. Let them not be conformed to the opinions of others but transformed by the renewing of their mind (Romans 12:2), knowing that Your will for them is perfect and pleasing.

Thank You, Lord, for Your faithfulness in turning rejection into redirection.

In Jesus' name, Amen.

A Prayer for School

Heavenly Father,
I come before You today with a heart full of gratitude for the opportunity my child(ren) has to learn and grow. I lift their school to You, asking for Your divine protection, guidance, and blessing over every aspect of it.

Your Word says in Proverbs 18:10:

> *"The name of the Lord is a strong tower: the righteous*
> *runneth into it, and is safe."*

I declare Your protection over the entire school campus—the staff, the students, and all who enter its doors. I plead the blood of Jesus over every classroom, hallway, and gathering space. Shield them, Father, from any plans of harm, especially from acts of violence or any form of danger.

In Jesus' name, I rebuke the spirit of fear and declare peace and safety. Let Your angels encamp around this school, as Your Word promises in Psalm 91:11:

*"For he shall give his angels charge over thee, to keep thee
in all thy ways."*

Lord, I pray for my child(ren)'s learning journey. Open their mind to understand and retain the knowledge taught to them. Your Word says in James 1:5:

*"If any of you lack wisdom, let him ask of God, that
giveth to all men liberally, and upbraideth not; and it
shall be given him."*

I ask for wisdom for my child(ren), their classmates, and their teachers. Remove every distraction that might hinder their focus or ability to learn. Help them to excel in their studies and to grow in confidence and understanding.

Father, I pray for the teachers, staff, and administration. Give them insight and creativity to teach children according to their unique needs and learning styles. May they be patient, compassionate, and wise in their instruction. Let them see the potential in every student and guide them with the love of Christ.

Finally, Lord, I pray for the atmosphere of the school. May it be filled with peace, unity, and respect. I bind every spirit of division, bullying, or negativity and replace it with love and encouragement. Let this school be a place where children thrive academically, emotionally, and spiritually.

Father, I trust You fully and believe You to be fully capable.
In Jesus' name, Amen.

A Prayer for Self-Worth

Heavenly Father,
I lay my child(ren) at Your feet, seeking Your direction, protection, and grace over their life. I thank You for the precious gift that they are and for the purpose You have placed on their life. Lord, as their parent, I pray that You guide them in understanding their identity in Christ and knowing how much they are valued by You.

Your Word says in Psalm 139:14:

> *"I will praise thee; for I am fearfully and wonderfully made: marvellous are thy works; and that my soul knoweth right well."*

Help my child(ren) to see themselves as You see them—created in Your image, full of purpose and worth. When the world tries to make them feel less than, remind them that their value comes from You alone and not from others' opinions. Let them walk confidently in the truth that they are Your masterpiece, created for good works (Ephesians 2:10).

Father, I pray for their heart and mind as they navigate the challenges of purity and relationships. Help them to honor their body as Your temple, as Your Word says in 1 Corinthians 6:19–20:

> *"What? know ye not that your body is the temple of the*
> *Holy Ghost which is in you, which ye have of God, and*
> *ye are not your own? For ye are bought with a price:*
> *therefore glorify God in your body, and in your spirit,*
> *which are God's."*

May they understand the beauty of purity and the blessings that come from living a life set apart for You.

Teach my child(ren) the benefits of waiting for marriage, Lord. Instill in them the understanding that Your plans for love and intimacy are holy and perfect. Remind them of Hebrews 13:4:

> *"Marriage is honourable in all, and the bed undefiled:*
> *but whoremongers and adulterers God will judge."*

Protect their heart from pressures and influences that go against Your design.

Surround them with godly mentors, friends, and leaders who will encourage them to live righteously. Help them to understand that waiting for marriage is not a restriction but a blessing that brings joy, security, and a deeper connection with You. Let them trust Your timing and believe that You will bring the right person into their life at the right time.

Above all, may my child's relationship with You be their greatest treasure. Let them find their worth, identity, and fulfillment in You alone.

Your Word says in Matthew 6:33:

> *"But seek ye first the kingdom of God, and his right-*
> *eousness; and all these things shall be added unto*
> *you."*

May they seek You first in all they do, and may their life glorify You in purity and love.

Thank You, Lord, for hearing my prayer. I trust You to guide my child and to protect their heart, mind, and body. I declare that they are Yours, and I pray that they walk in the fullness of Your love and purpose.

In Jesus' mighty name, Amen.

A Prayer for Their
Future Spouse

Oh, Gracious Father,
I come before You with a heart of faith, lifting up my child(ren)'s future spouse to You. Lord, You know the plans You have for my child(ren)—plans for good and not for harm, to give them a hope and a future (Jeremiah 29:11). I trust that Your plans include a godly spouse who will love, honor, and cherish them according to Your will.

Father, I pray that my child(ren)'s future spouse will have a deep and abiding love for You. Let them be someone who seeks You with their whole heart. May their union bring them both closer to You, unlocking new depths of spiritual growth. May they build their lives on the solid foundation of Christ and walk in obedience to Your Word.

Lord, I ask that their future spouse be a person of integrity, humility, and self-awareness. Help them to know who they are in You and to live with purpose and authenticity. Your Word says in Proverbs 4:23:

> *"Keep thy heart with all diligence; for out of it are the issues of life."*

Teach them to guard their heart and grow in wisdom, so they can enter into marriage prepared to love and serve selflessly.

I pray that this person You have ordained to cover them will add to my child(ren)'s life and never lead them away from You. Let them be a partner who encourages my child(ren) in their faith, helps them grow spiritually, and strengthens their relationship with You.

As Ecclesiastes 4:9–10 says:

> *"Two are better than one; because they have a good reward*
> *for their labour. For if they fall, the one will lift up his*
> *fellow: but woe to him that is alone when he falleth;*
> *for he hath not another to help him up."*

May their relationship be one of mutual support, encouragement, and love that reflects Christ's love for the church.

Lord, I also ask for purity and faithfulness in their lives as they wait for each other. Protect them from distractions and temptations. Help them to walk in holiness and prepare their hearts, minds, and spirits for the sacred covenant of marriage.

Lastly, Father, I pray that this person will be someone who displays the fruit of the Spirit. May they be a person of prayer, faith, and unwavering trust in You.

Thank You for Your faithfulness. May their union bring glory to the Kingdom of God.

In Jesus' name, Amen.

A Prayer Against Perversion

Heavenly Father,

    I come before You today, lifting my child(ren) to Your throne of grace. Thank You for the precious gift of their lives and for entrusting them to my care. I stand on Your Word and denounce every spirit of perversion, impurity, and ungodliness that seeks to influence or harm them.

Lord, I declare that my child(ren) belong to You. As Your Word says in Proverbs 22:6:

> *"Train up a child in the way he should go: and when he is old, he will not depart from it."*

I commit to raising them in Your truth and exposing any corruption in their heart, mind, or body.

Your Word declares in 2 Timothy 1:7:

> *"For God hath not given us the spirit of fear; but of power, and of love, and of a sound mind."*

I proclaim that my child(ren) have sound minds and hearts aligned with Your will. Let every ungodly influence or attempt of the enemy to twist or distort their thinking be completely broken in Jesus' name.

Father, I declare Psalm 101:3 over my child(ren):

> *"I will set no wicked thing before mine eyes."*

May their eyes, ears, and heart be guarded from every form of impurity and anything that does not glorify You. Protect them from exposure to harmful images, words, and actions that could lead them astray.

I renounce every assignment of the enemy to plant seeds of perversion in their lives. Your Word says in James 4:7:

> *"Submit yourselves therefore to God. Resist the devil, and he will flee from you."*

I submit my child(ren) and family to You, Lord, and I command every demonic influence to flee in the name of Jesus.

Lord, I ask that You fill my child(ren) with Your Holy Spirit. Let the fruits of the Spirit—love, joy, peace, patience, kindness, goodness, faithfulness, gentleness, and self-control—grow within them daily (Galatians 5:22–23). May they be strengthened to walk in purity and righteousness all the days of their lives.

I declare Your promise from Isaiah 54:13:

> *"And all thy children shall be taught of the Lord; and great shall be the peace of thy children."*

Teach them, Lord, and fill their hearts with Your truth and wisdom. I pray that their identities will be firmly rooted in You and that they will know they are fearfully and wonderfully made.

Father, I seal this prayer in the mighty name of Jesus, claiming Your protection, guidance, and purity over my child(ren). May they walk boldly in Your light, free from the grip of perversion, and live lives that honor and glorify You.

In Jesus' name, Amen.

A Prayer for My Children's Children

Heavenly Father,
    I come before You today with a heart full of gratitude for the gift of my child(ren) and the generations that will come after them. Lord, I thank You for the blessing of grandchildren and the legacy You are building through our bloodline.

Your Word says in Psalm 127:3:

> *"Lo, children are an heritage of the Lord: and the fruit of the womb is his reward."*

Lord, I pray over my child(ren) and the children they will one day bring into this world. I ask that You prepare their hearts, minds, and spirits to raise these grandchildren in the fear and knowledge of the Lord. May they teach them Your ways and guide them to walk in righteousness.

Proverbs 22:6 declares:

> *"Train up a child in the way he should go: and when he is old, he will not depart from it."*

Let this promise be fulfilled in my family, Lord.

Father, I lift up my bloodline to You. I thank You for the work You are doing to purify and cleanse it from generational sin, curses, and anything that does not reflect Your holiness. Let my grandchildren and future generations continue this work, carrying out the mission and calling You have placed on our family.

Your Word says in Exodus 20:6:

> *"And shewing mercy unto thousands of them that love me, and keep my commandments."*

Let Your love and faithfulness rest upon our bloodline for generations to come.

I declare Isaiah 54:17 over them:

> *"No weapon that is formed against thee shall prosper."*

Guard their hearts, minds, and bodies, and place a hedge of protection around them. Cover them with the blood of Jesus, and let Your angels encamp around them (Psalm 91:11).

Father, may my grandchildren and future generations carry out the mission You have placed on our bloodline. Let them be bold in faith, strong in character, and unwavering in their love for You.

As Luke 1:50 says:

> *"And his mercy is on them that fear him from generation to generation."*

I stand on this promise, knowing that my family is covered by Your power and protection.

In Jesus' mighty name, Amen.

About the Author

Win Dockery is a devoted wife, mother of six, and founder of *Journey with Grace and Mercy LLC*, a mission-driven business that combines hand-crafted pearl bracelets with a transformative mentoring program for young girls. With a heart anchored in faith and a life refined by both personal and spiritual battles, Win has emerged as a passionate voice for women, families, and the next generation.

Through her writing and mentoring, she empowers women to pray with boldness, live with intention, and rise with purpose. *War Mother* was birthed from Win's own journey—a sacred call to intercede, protect, and nurture her family in a world that often wages war against faith and identity. Her words are a clarion call to mothers everywhere: your prayers are powerful, your presence is purposeful, and you are never alone in the battle.

facebook.com/TheDockeryFamily

instagram.com/jwgam_princesswarriors

www.ingramcontent.com/pod-product-compliance
Lightning Source LLC
Chambersburg PA
CBHW051244120626
46547CB00014B/1787